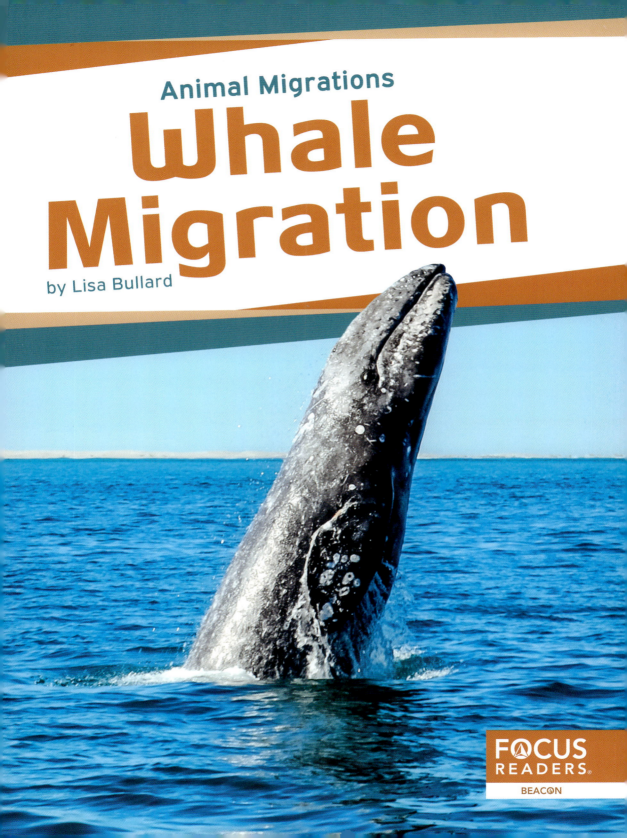

Animal Migrations
Whale Migration

by Lisa Bullard

www.focusreaders.com

Copyright © 2024 by Focus Readers®, Lake Elmo, MN 55042. All rights reserved. No part of this book may be reproduced or utilized in any form or by any means without written permission from the publisher.

Focus Readers is distributed by North Star Editions:
sales@northstareditions.com | 888-417-0195

Produced for Focus Readers by Red Line Editorial.

Photographs ©: Shutterstock Images, cover, 1, 8, 11, 13, 16, 21, 29; iStockphoto, 4, 7, 14–15, 18, 24, 27; Bryan & Cherry Alexander/Science Source, 22

Library of Congress Cataloging-in-Publication Data
Names: Bullard, Lisa, author.
Title: Whale migration / by Lisa Bullard.
Description: Lake Elmo, MN : Focus Readers, [2024] | Series: Animal
  migrations | Includes index. | Audience: Grades 2-3
Identifiers: LCCN 2023001182 (print) | LCCN 2023001183 (ebook) | ISBN
  9781637396100 (hardcover) | ISBN 9781637396674 (paperback) | ISBN
  9781637397787 (pdf) | ISBN 9781637397244 (ebook)
Subjects: LCSH: Whales--Migration--Juvenile literature. | Whales--Juvenile
  literature.
Classification: LCC QL737.C4 B8635 2024 (print) | LCC QL737.C4 (ebook) |
  DDC 599.5--dc23/eng/20230223
LC record available at https://lccn.loc.gov/2023001182
LC ebook record available at https://lccn.loc.gov/2023001183

Printed in the United States of America
Mankato, MN
082023

About the Author

Lisa Bullard is the author of more than 100 books for children, including the mystery novel *Turn Left at the Cow*. She also teaches writing classes for adults and children. Lisa grew up in Minnesota and now lives just north of Minneapolis.

Table of Contents

CHAPTER 1
The Great Gray Migration 5

CHAPTER 2
Baleen Whales 9

ANIMAL SPOTLIGHT
North and South 14

CHAPTER 3
Toothed Whales 17

CHAPTER 4
Arctic Migrators 23

Focus on Whale Migration • 28
Glossary • 30
To Learn More • 31
Index • 32

Chapter 1

The Great Gray Migration

A gray whale swims in the cold waters near Alaska. Summer is her time to gain more weight. There is plenty to eat in this area. But in the fall, the waters become icier. It is time to **migrate**.

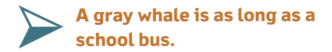
A gray whale is as long as a school bus.

The gray whale starts swimming south. Her journey takes more than two months. When it is done, she has traveled about 5,000 miles (8,000 km).

The whale gives birth in the warm waters near Mexico. In late winter, she leads her **calf** north. They

Each summer day, a gray whale eats more than 2,000 pounds (910 kg) of food.

 Sea animals called barnacles sometimes live on whales' bodies.

swim back to the **Arctic**. When fall returns, both whales will travel south again.

Chapter 2

Baleen Whales

Some animals change their home during different times of year. This is called migration. Many whales migrate long distances.

There are two major types of whales. The first is baleen whales.

 Humpback whales can travel more than 10,000 miles (16,000 km) each year.

These whales do not have teeth. Instead, they have **bristles**. The bristles act like filters. Water goes in and out, but food stays in.

This group includes blue whales and fin whales. Gray whales and humpbacks are also baleen whales. These two whales make the longest migrations of any **mammal**.

Fun Fact

Blue whales are the largest animals that have ever lived.

 A humpback whale opens its mouth wide.

Many baleen whales have similar migrations. In the summer, they feed in **polar** waters. There is plenty of food available. But over time, the weather grows colder. The whales move closer to the **equator**.

11

Their calves are born in these warmer waters.

Scientists are not completely sure why baleen whales migrate. Different experts have different answers. Some believe warmer waters are safer for calves. Young whales may be less likely to be killed by **predators** there. Other experts note that calves do not have much fat. They might need the warmer water to keep from getting cold.

 A young humpback whale swims with its parent.

Whales cannot find enough food in warm waters. So, they swim back to the poles for summer. They eat a lot. They have to get ready for another migration.

ANIMAL SPOTLIGHT

North and South

Humpback whales swim through oceans around the world. But humpbacks in southern and northern waters never meet. That is because their seasons are reversed. The southern summer is the northern winter.

The humpbacks head south around the same time. The northern humpbacks leave the Arctic. They swim toward the equator for winter. The southern humpbacks travel south, too. They spend their summer feeding near Antarctica. Months later, both groups swim north. They never cross paths.

Many whales travel in groups called pods.

Chapter 3

Toothed Whales

Toothed whales are the second major type of whales. These whales are hunters. So, they have teeth to bite **prey**. Some toothed whales do not migrate. Others do. Their migration patterns vary.

Sperm whales eat squid, fish, and other sea creatures.

 A male sperm whale can weigh more than 100,000 pounds (45,000 kg).

Sperm whales are the largest toothed whale. Females and their young stay in warmer waters all

18

year. But adult males migrate to colder waters. Scientists are not sure why.

Baird's beaked whales spend summer and fall close to shore. They migrate in winter and spring. They spend those seasons in the deep ocean. Again, scientists do not know why.

Killer whales are another type of toothed whale. Some killer whales migrate along with their prey. For example, they may follow salmon.

Killer whales usually stay in colder water. But sometimes they head to warmer waters. After that, they quickly return to colder waters. The journey can cover nearly 7,000 miles (11,300 km).

Killer whales **molt** in the warm water. That way, they do not lose body heat. Molting helps them stay

Killer whales are a kind of dolphin. All dolphins are toothed whales.

 Like most whales, killer whales can jump out of the water. This behavior is called breaching.

healthy. And it might explain why killer whales migrate.

Scientists continue to study molting. They want to know if that is why other whales migrate.

Chapter 4

Arctic Migrators

Many whales visit the far north. But three kinds of whales stay there all year. One is the bowhead. This is a baleen whale. The other two are belugas and narwhals. They are both toothed whales.

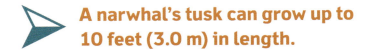
A narwhal's tusk can grow up to 10 feet (3.0 m) in length.

 Beluga whales are known for their all-white color.

These whales migrate from one part of the Arctic to another. They might travel 1,000 miles (1,600 km) in a year. Ice affects their migrations.

24

In the summer, belugas stay along the coasts. They gather in shallow, warmer water. That is where they molt. When the weather grows cold, these waters get covered in ice. The belugas migrate. They swim offshore. They find open areas within the sea ice. That is where they spend winters.

Narwhals spend summers along Arctic coasts. Then winter comes. The water turns to solid ice. The narwhals migrate farther south.

Ice fills these waters, too. But the ice has cracks and holes in it. The narwhals can reach the surface to breathe. Winter is also when narwhals feed. Their prey is deep under the ice.

The ice also guides bowhead whale migration. The ice changes

Fun Fact

Narwhals may dive more than 1 mile (1.6 km) deep. They can hold their breath for 25 minutes.

 A bowhead whale swims in the cold waters off the coast of Greenland.

with the seasons. Bowhead whales follow the ice's changing edge.

Scientists still have lots to learn about all whales. They continue to study their lives and migration. They want to understand these amazing animals.

FOCUS ON
Whale Migration

Write your answers on a separate piece of paper.

1. Explain the main ideas of Chapter 3.

2. Which kind of whale do you find most interesting? Why?

3. Which type of whale is a baleen whale?
   - **A.** narwhal
   - **B.** killer whale
   - **C.** gray whale

4. What might happen if a whale is trapped under a big area of ice with no cracks?
   - **A.** The whale would hold its breath until the ice melts.
   - **B.** The whale could eventually die from lack of air.
   - **C.** The whale would keep breathing underneath the ice.

5. What does **filters** mean in this book?

*The bristles act like **filters**. Water goes in and out, but food stays in.*

  A. objects that strain water to trap certain items
  B. types of whales that migrate long distances
  C. types of food that are easy for whales to find

6. What does **reversed** mean in this book?

*That is because their seasons are **reversed**. The southern summer is the northern winter.*

  A. opposite
  B. similar
  C. very hot

Answer key on page 32.

Glossary

Arctic
The most northern part of Earth.

bristles
Stiff, hair-like parts that look like brushes.

calf
A baby or young whale.

equator
An imaginary line that runs around the middle of Earth.

mammal
An animal that has hair and produces milk for its young.

migrate
To move from one region to another.

molt
To lose an outer layer of skin so that a new layer can grow.

polar
Having to do with areas near the North Pole or South Pole.

predators
Animals that hunt other animals for food.

prey
Animals that are hunted and eaten by other animals.

To Learn More

BOOKS

Forrester, Philippa. *Amazing Animal Journeys: The Most Incredible Migrations in the Natural World.* New York: DK Publishing, 2023.

London, Martha. *Looking into the Ocean*. Mankato, MN: The Child's World, 2020.

Murray, Julie. *Beluga Whales*. Minneapolis: Abdo Publishing, 2020.

NOTE TO EDUCATORS

Visit **www.focusreaders.com** to find lesson plans, activities, links, and other resources related to this title.

Index

A
Alaska, 5
Arctic, 7, 14, 24–25

B
baleen whales, 9–13, 23
belugas, 23, 25
blue whales, 10
bowhead whales, 23,
    26–27

C
calves, 6, 12

G
gray whales, 5–7, 10

H
humpback whales, 10, 14

K
killer whales, 19–21

M
Mexico, 6

N
narwhals, 23–26

P
predators, 12
prey, 17, 19, 26

S
sperm whales, 18–19

T
toothed whales, 17–21,
    23–25

Answer Key: 1. Answers will vary; **2.** Answers will vary; **3.** C; **4.** B; **5.** A; **6.** A